Kids C
SAFE!

Katacha Díaz

Kids ride bikes.
Kids use helmets.

Kids look for cars.

Kids look left.

Kids look right.

5

Kids ride in cars.
Kids use seat belts.

Kids look for signs.

Kids stop.

Kids go.

Kids listen
to Mom and Dad.

Kids listen
to the firefighter.

SQUAD CO.1

788

SQUAD CO.1

13

Kids listen
to the police officer.

Kids can be safe!